Study Guide:

The Hate U Give

Deluxe Edition

Study Guides and Lesson Plans

By: Dr. Vincent Verret

Description

Welcome to the best Study Guide for The Hate U Give with this special Deluxe Edition, featuring over 100 pages of guided activities, diagrams, visual organizers, note-taking exercises, and essential questions! With sections aimed at citing evidence from the text, this study guide for The Hate U Give is up to date with Next Generation, 21st Century, and Common Core skill requirements. This study guide for The Hate U Give can be used as BOTH a study guide for readers/students AND an instructional guide for teachers. It is the perfect companion to introducing literature in any classroom!

Master the material and ace any assignment with this innovative study guide series. This book is perfect for both students and teachers, as it produces true mastery of content knowledge and book details.

Other study guides for The Hate U Give simply give basic details of the novel, meaning that students read over material without digesting or learning it. Other study guides take complex themes, concepts, and information and just regurgitate it to readers.

But, this Study Guide for The Hate U Give is different. Using the original text as a guide, you will learn to cite evidence from the text in order to complete and reflect on your reading. Readers will self-generate additional notes within the structure provided by this Study Guide.

Designed by a veteran educator, this study guide for The Hate U Give GUIDES the learner to discovering the answers for themselves, creating a fully detailed study guide in the user's own words. Filled with guided reading activities, students are able to fill this guidebook with their own information.

If you read it, write it, and reflect on it, you will learn it!

Teachers: Besides being a great lesson plan or activity resource, you can also purchase a set of these books (or one book and make copies) for your entire class. It makes the perfect guided reading activity for The Hate U Give and will teach students how to internalize the reading, note taking, and learning process that advanced readers naturally perform. These make the perfect workbook to keep your class engaged and learning!

Instructions for Use

This study guide for The Hate U Give is **designed as a guided reading workbook**. Keep the study guide open and next to you while you read. The sections are sequential, and allow you to annotate (a fancy word for taking notes). As you read the book, continue to take notes within this guide. Once you finish, you'll have a complete study guide, IN YOUR OWN WORDS.

The fact is, that actually taking notes and then reading them, means that you learn while you take the notes, it's easier to read since it is in your own words, AND you will actually master the material since you have experienced it in multiple ways (reading AND writing).

If you are a general reader, I want to call your attention towards our sections on annotating and analysis.

As a student, I want you to focus on writing your own annotations and using these activities for your own understanding.

For teachers, I have included specific activities for you to try with your classes. You have my permission, as a fellow educator, to purchase multiple books (I appreciate your support) OR feel free to purchase a book, make copies for your class, (and please recommend the book to others)

I hope you enjoy this study guide!

The Hate U Give Annotation Guide

Don't be alarmed! Annotation is simply a fancy way of saying "taking notes". As you read a text, you should always take the time to jot down some notes.

You should break your notes down into two categories: descriptive and understanding.

Descriptive notes are the most simple. When making descriptive annotations, you are writing down basic summaries of whatever you are reading. A descriptive annotation may include notes about the plot and setting.

These notes help you remember what is occurring and are mostly used for you to quickly review materials. These types of notes are especially helpful in books that have characters that move in and out of the story. In a non-fiction book, your descriptive notes should summarize and explain basic themes and topics so that you can quickly analyze these components later.

Understanding annotations are notes taken to help you explain the connections between actions or plot points. In particular, you should take notes based on a character's motives or any reasons to their actions. This can help you understand the flow of The Hate U Give and its plot.

Additional Journal Pages for Annotating are given to you at the back of this book. Happy annotating!

The Hate U Give First Impression: What's in a Name?

Before you begin reading, take a look at the name of your book. What does it mean to you? What does it make you expect when you read? Does it catch your attention? What emotions does it draw out?

Reflect on these questions and answer them below (as well as any additional thoughts). Once you finish the book, come back to this page and see if your predictions were correct!

Predictions:

When you finish the book, use this space to reflect on your initial impressions. Were they correct? How was the book different from what you expected?

_____

_____

_____

_____

_____

_____

_____

_____

_____

_____

_____

_____

_____

The Hate U Give Character Analysis

As each character appears, turn to this section and record the information below. Fill in as much as you can from the first appearance of the character.

Remember, authors describe characters intentionally, certain physical descriptions are actually descriptions of how the character will act. Sometimes this is very direct, and other times, authors enjoy intentionally defying stereotypes. The last question in each character analysis, should be addressed AFTER you have finished reading the book.

I have left sections for multiple characters.

Character Name: _____
_____

Is this Character a Main Character or a Supporting Character? _____
_____

Physical Appearance: _____
_____
_____
_____
_____
_____

Personality: _____
_____
_____
_____
_____
_____

Important Actions and How they Impact the Plot

_____
_____
_____
_____
_____
_____
_____

Motivations / Reasons Behind their Behavior:

_____
_____
_____
_____
_____
_____
_____

Post-Reading Character Reflection:

Did this character change in any of these key areas by the conclusion of the book? How and why?

Behavior
_____
_____
_____
_____

Motives
_____
_____
_____

Relationships to Other Characters
_____
_____
_____
_____

Character Name: _____
_____

Is this Character a Main Character or a Supporting Character? _____
_____

Physical Appearance: _____
_____
_____
_____
_____
_____
_____

Personality: _____
_____
_____
_____
_____
_____
_____

Important Actions and How they Impact the Plot

_____
_____
_____
_____
_____
_____
_____
_____
_____

Motivations / Reasons Behind their Behavior:

_____
_____
_____
_____
_____
_____
_____
_____

Post-Reading Character Reflection:

Did this character change in any of these key areas by the conclusion of the book? How and why?

Behavior
_____
_____
_____
_____

Motives
_____
_____
_____

Relationships to Other Characters
_____
_____
_____

Character Name: _____

_____

Is this Character a Main Character or a Supporting Character? _____

_____

Physical Appearance: _____

_____
_____
_____
_____
_____
_____

Personality: _____

_____
_____
_____
_____
_____
_____

Important Actions and How they Impact the Plot

_____
_____
_____
_____
_____
_____
_____
_____
_____

Motivations / Reasons Behind their Behavior:

_____
_____
_____
_____
_____
_____
_____
_____

Post-Reading Character Reflection:

Did this character change in any of these key areas by the conclusion of the book? How and why?

Behavior _____
_____
_____
_____

Motives _____
_____
_____

Relationships to Other Characters _____
_____
_____
_____

Character Name: _____
_____

Is this Character a Main Character or a Supporting Character? _____
_____

Physical Appearance: _____
_____
_____
_____
_____
_____
_____

Personality: _____
_____
_____
_____
_____
_____
_____

Important Actions and How they Impact the Plot

_____
_____
_____
_____
_____
_____
_____
_____
_____

Motivations / Reasons Behind their Behavior:

_____
_____
_____
_____
_____
_____
_____
_____

Post-Reading Character Reflection:

Did this character change in any of these key areas by the conclusion of the book? How and why?

Behavior
_____
_____
_____
_____

Motives
_____
_____
_____

Relationships to Other Characters
_____
_____
_____
_____

Character Name: _____
_____

Is this Character a Main Character or a Supporting Character? _____
_____

Physical Appearance: _____
_____
_____
_____
_____
_____

Personality: _____
_____
_____
_____
_____
_____
_____

Important Actions and How they Impact the Plot

_____
_____
_____
_____
_____
_____
_____
_____

Motivations / Reasons Behind their Behavior:

_____
_____
_____
_____
_____
_____
_____
_____

Post-Reading Character Reflection:

Did this character change in any of these key areas by the conclusion of the book? How and why?

Behavior
_____
_____
_____

Motives
_____
_____
_____

Relationships to Other Characters
_____
_____
_____

The Hate U Give Setting Notes

Now it is time to discuss the different settings or physical environments in each novel. Physical environments frame the story, set the mood, and provide historical context. Often, the setting of a novel is used to reinforce a character's behavior or traits.

Often times, the setting of a book will change, so I've left you multiple spaces to discuss the setting.

1st Setting:
_____

Time and Place:
_____

Descriptive Details:
_____
_____
_____
_____

Mood Created / Emotional Response:
_____
_____
_____
_____

How does the setting influence the characters?
_____
_____
_____
_____

2nd Setting:
_____

Time and Place:
_____

Descriptive Details:
_____
_____
_____
_____

Mood Created / Emotional Response:
_____
_____
_____
_____

How does the setting influence the characters?
_____
_____
_____
_____

3rd Setting:
_____

Time and Place:
_____

Descriptive Details:
_____
_____
_____
_____

Mood Created / Emotional Response:
_____
_____
_____
_____

How does the setting influence the characters?
_____
_____
_____
_____

4th Setting:
_____

Time and Place:
_____

Descriptive Details:
_____
_____
_____
_____

Mood Created / Emotional Response:
_____
_____
_____
_____

How does the setting influence the characters?
_____
_____
_____

5th Setting:
_____

Time and Place:
_____

Descriptive Details:
_____
_____
_____
_____

Mood Created / Emotional Response:
_____
_____
_____
_____

How does the setting influence the characters?
_____
_____
_____
_____

The Hate U Give Plot Outline and Study Guide

In this section, we will outline the entire book using a listing technique. You should write down each action, change in setting, or important character development, in the following pages.

Afterwards, we will use this information to analyze and understand the major conflict of the book, it's theme, and lessons.

I will provide a few pages of lists, every reader is different, so you may choose to list more or less events. Do not feel like you have to complete the list by using all the numbered spaces.

The Hate U Give Major Plot Outline:

1.
2.
3.
4.
5.
6.
7.
8.
9.
10.
11.
12.
13.
14.
15.
16.

17.
18.
19.
20.
21.
22.
23.
24.
25.
26.
27.
28.
29.
30.
31.
32.
33.

34.
35.
36.
37.
38.
39.
40.
41.
42.
43.
44.
45.
46.
47.
48.
49.
50.

51. _____
52. _____
53. _____
54. _____
55. _____
56. _____
57. _____
58. _____
59. _____
60. _____
61. _____
62. _____
63. _____
64. _____
65. _____
66. _____
67. _____

68. _____
69. _____
70. _____
71. _____
72. _____
73. _____
74. _____
75. _____
76. _____
77. _____
78. _____
79. _____
80. _____
81. _____
82. _____
83. _____
84. _____

85.

Conclusion / Ending:

The Hate U Give Ending Questions

These questions allow you to check your outline. If you cannot answer any of these questions, you need to add more detail to your outline or reread the book (hint: you aren't taking enough notes on the important details).

Remember, it isn't how fast you can read. Part of this guided study guide is to force you to slow down and read the material deliberately, so that you can LEARN the details.

1. How does the main character change over the course of the book? Cite specific physical, mental, and morality changes.

_____
_____
_____
_____
_____
_____
_____
_____
_____
_____
_____
_____
_____
_____
_____
_____
_____
_____
_____
_____
_____
_____
_____
_____

2. What is the main character's initial goal or motivation? Does this change during the story? How does their goal change?

_____
_____
_____
_____
_____
_____
_____
_____
_____
_____
_____
_____
_____
_____
_____
_____
_____
_____
_____
_____
_____
_____
_____

3. Name one character and how they HELP the main character achieve their goals or deal with conflicts.

4. Name one character and how they try to STOP the main character from achieving their goals or dealing with a conflict.

5. How does the environment (both physical and political) help or hinder the main character and their goals?

_____
_____
_____
_____
_____
_____
_____
_____
_____
_____
_____
_____
_____
_____
_____
_____
_____
_____
_____
_____
_____
_____
_____
_____
_____

6. What is the climax of the book? How does the climax intensify the conflict of the book? What is the resolution of the conflict?

The Hate U Give Section Summary

First, read back over your plot outline, and then the answers to the ending questions. Now I want you to mentally divide the book up into sections.

Introduction: the initial section where characters and setting are introduced. You will get the first indication of an issue or problem that needs to be solved.

Rising Action: how does the problem impact the characters, and how do the characters act to solve this issue? At this stage in the plot, the characters will often fail to solve the problem.

Conclusion: Finally the problem is solved or the characters are no longer able to solve the issue (and are defeated by it). Either way, the book is now resolved.

For each of these sections, on the following pages, write your own summary. This summary should go beyond your outline, and also include some analysis of the characters and their involvement. Specifically, how does the main character(s) inteact with the story's problem/plot, etc. Remember, characters are BOTH influenced by and have influence on the plot, setting, and other characters.

Introduction Summary:

Rising Action Summary:

_____

_____

_____

_____

_____

_____

_____

_____

_____

_____

_____

_____

_____

Conclusion Summary:

The Hate U Give Theme Analysis

A theme is the major lesson or message that the author is trying to teach/tell us. All books have a purpose or try to give meaning to an idea. Reflect on the your previous plot outline. How did the author use the events in this book to teach lesson or convey a message? Are there multiple lessons to learn?

Theme:

How does the author teacher us this theme?

How does this theme change the characters?

The Hate U Give Additional Activities

At this point, if you've followed all of my instructions, you will have a solid study guide that can be used to prepare for any exam.

However, I wanted to include some additional activities for you. The activities on the following pages allow for advanced understanding and new ways to learn material (beyond writing guided notes).

Teachers, each of these activities can become a great activity. Use them as a writing prompt or to replace more traditional worksheets.

The Hate U Give Close Reading

Select a portion of the text, preferably one that is rich in detail. Reread this text, slowly and closely. Write detailed notes on each paragraph explaining the character's motives, the message being presented by the author, and the importance of the text in the plot.

Text:

Close Reading Notes:

The Hate U Give Character Mapping

All characters or ideas connected have a clear relationship with each other. For some books, this mapping is easy because many characters are related to each other.

However, a family map of characters is often too simple. Make a map or diagram of interactions and feelings that connect characters. For example, you can map out how the actions of one character impact another character.

These maps are very useful in keep track of characters and their relationships in some author's works, such as Jane Austen, who has multiple characters that come in and out of the plot at various stages.

I've given you some samples to use on the following pages.

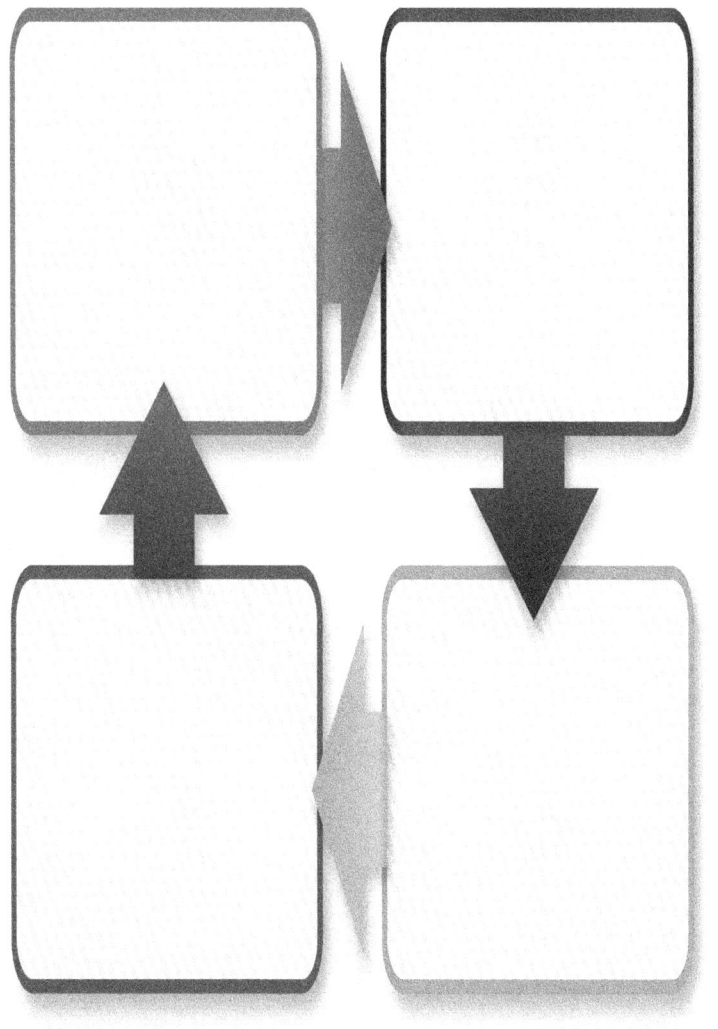

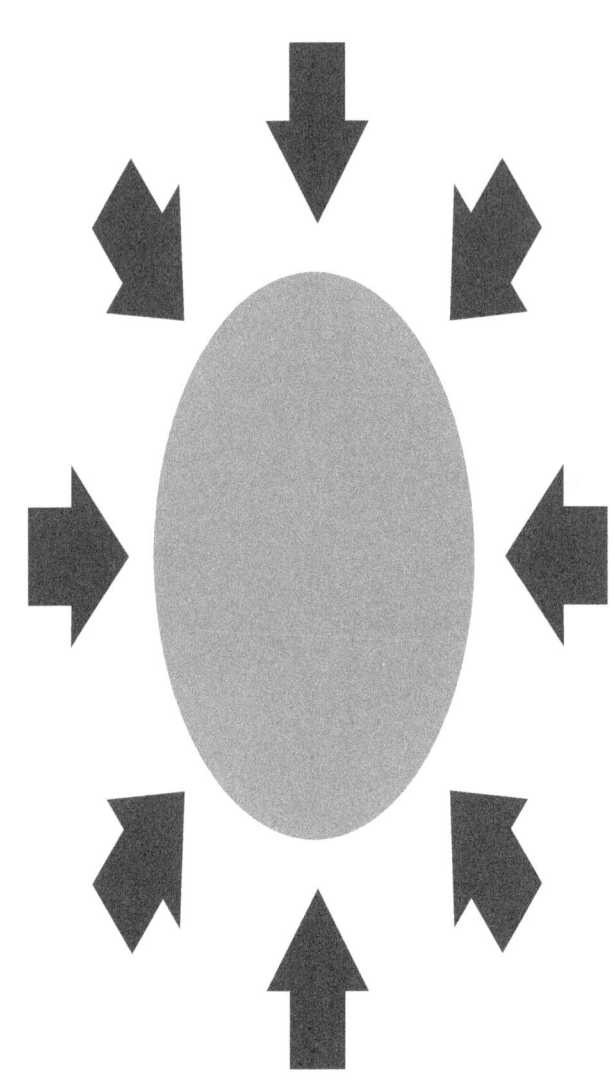

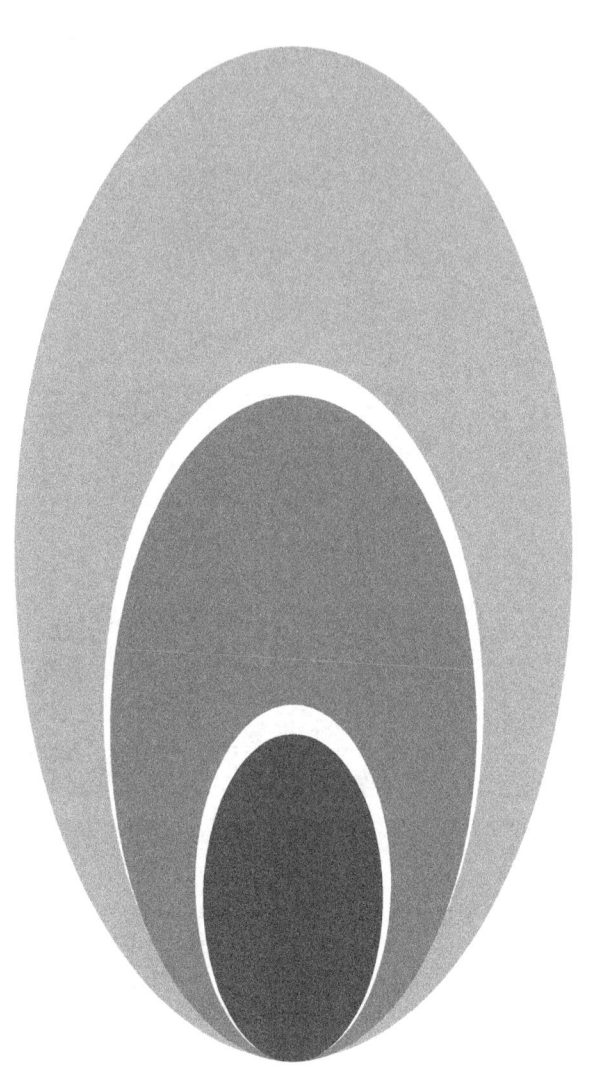

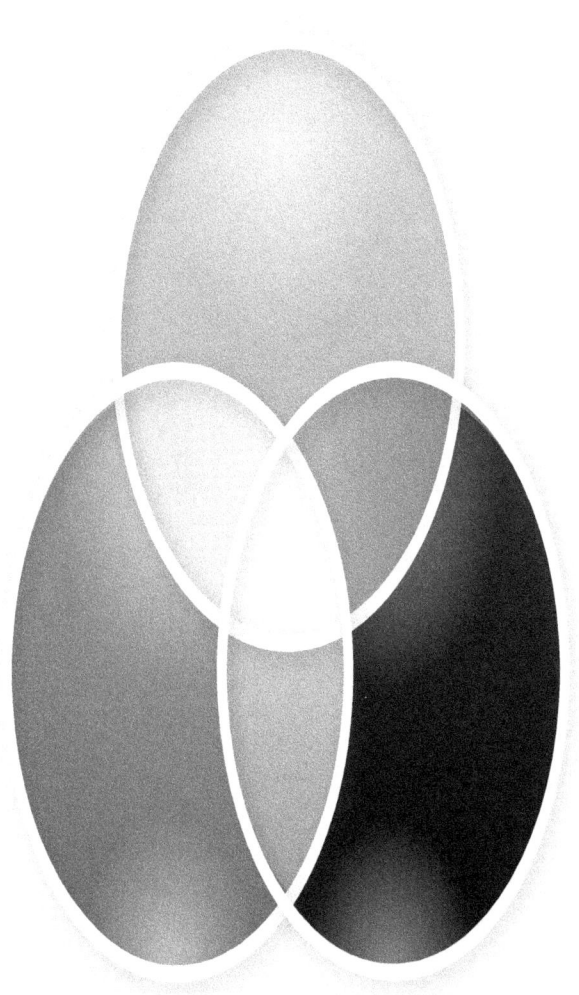

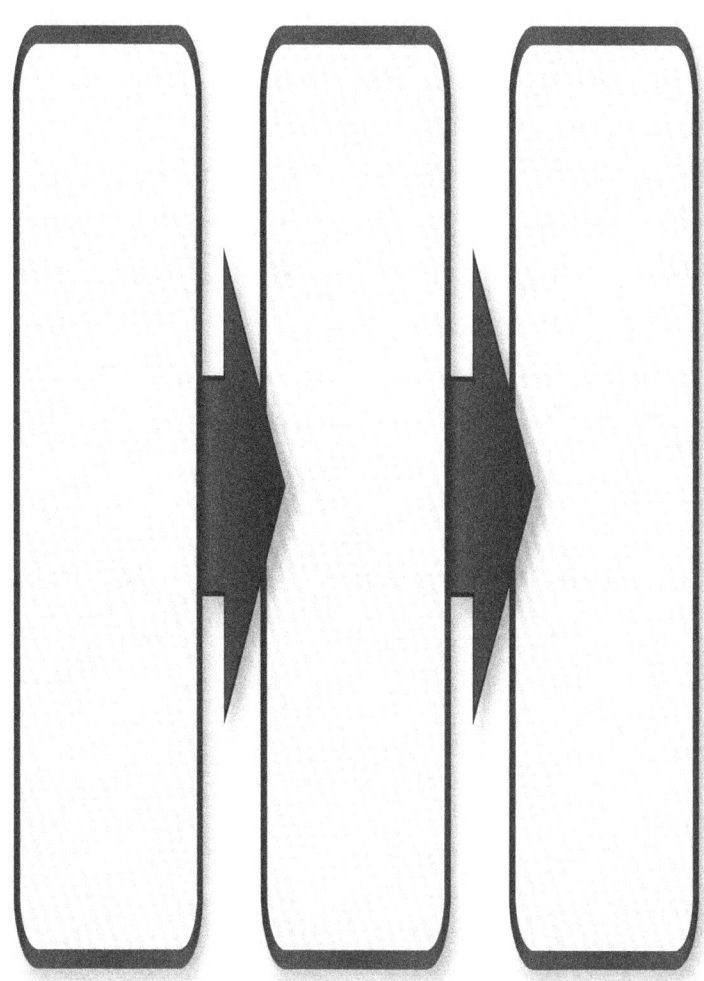

The Hate U Give Character Analysis

From your character mapping activity, focus on one character that you are interested in, with the protagonist or antagonist being an excellent choice. Write an essay describing the character, their role through the plot, and how they change. When writing, focus on the initial introduction of the character and how their changes relate to the theme/lessons/plot of the work. Use any descriptors that the author uses, and cite specific examples from the text.

On the following page is a sample essay excerpt.

Excerpt:

The general impression is that he was a once great and promising man who was betrayed. Through betrayal, he lost everything. He lives on through life as a loner and a miser. He then suffers even more when he loses his last love, money. Luckily for him a young child, described as a young angel, saves his life. Afterwards, he changes again back into a promising person, missing only his youth. His miserly and miserable life should not be imitated, but for all those in trouble, down on their luck or in depression his change should be looked upon with hope for the change that the future brings.

The Hate U Give Character Analysis

The Hate U Give Timeline

You can also make a timeline of events or ideas in the book. Pay close attention to the cause and effect that this timeline displays.

In terms of the plot, you can start with a single action and trace the consequences of that one action throughout the plot.

Choose an action by one of the characters near the beginning of the story, such as a chance encounter with another character, and trace this action's impact on the rest of the plot. Often times, there is a single action that pushes the plot into motion and maintains suspense/momentum within a story.

The Hate U Give Thematic Essay

Select a central theme, idea, or word and discuss its importance and meaning within the larger story. In order to fully understand the author's intent, it is useful to search for a repeated word or theme.

For example, in Shakespeare, the word and image of "Blood" is repeated throughout the play. Thus, you could write an essay exploring the importance of Blood, using examples from the test to show how the author draws upon the text to strengthen their argument that "Blood" is a central theme and an intentional imagery within the play.

The Hate U Give Thematic Essay

Thank you!

Reader,

Please allow me to extend my heartfelt thank you to you for purchasing this book. As an educator, your purchase allows me to earn additional revenue for my family, while helping others learn amazing classic works or a new subject. Thank you so much for your purchase, I truly appreciate you.

Sincerely,

Dr. Vincent Verret

If you are looking for more books, check my author page on amazon:

https://www.amazon.com/Vincent-Verret/e/B01B8E0A1K

or just search "Vincent Verret"

Additional Annotating Pages:

CPSIA information can be obtained
at www.ICGtesting.com
Printed in the USA
BVHW041144270319
543855BV00007B/65/P